HEINEMANN GUIDED READERS

INTERMEDIATE LEVEL

W. SOMERSET MAUGHAM

Footprints in the Jungle and Other Stories

Retold by Rod Sinclair

Illustrated by Fermin Rocker

HEINEMANN

INTERMEDIATE LEVEL

Series Editor: John Milne

The Heinemann Guided Readers provide a choice of enjoyable reading material for learners of English. The series is published at five levels – Starter, Beginner, Elementary, Intermediate and Upper. At **Intermediate Level**, the control of content and language has the following main features:

Information Control

Information which is vital to the understanding of the story is presented in an easily assimilated manner and is repeated when necessary. Difficult allusion and metaphor are avoided and cultural backgrounds are made explicit.

Structure Control

Most of the structures used in the Readers will be familiar to students who have completed an elementary course of English. Other grammatical features may occur, but their use is made clear through context and reinforcement. This ensures that the reading, as well as being enjoyable, provides a continual learning situation for the students. Sentences are limited in most cases to a maximum of three clauses and within sentences there is a balanced use of adverbial and adjectival phrases. Great care is taken with pronoun reference.

Vocabulary Control

There is a basic vocabulary of approximately 1,600 words. Help is given to the students in the form of illustrations, which are closely related to the text.

Glossary

Some difficult words and phrases in this book are important for understanding the story. Some of these words are explained in the story, some are shown in the pictures, and others are marked with a number like this . . .[3] Words with a number are explained in the Glossary on page 61.

Contents

A Note About the Author

William Somerset Maugham is one of the most famous British writers.

Maugham was born in Paris in 1874. He studied medicine to become a doctor. His first book, called *Lisa of Lambeth*, was published in 1896. It was successful and many copies were sold.

Maugham decided not to work as a doctor, but to be a writer instead. He wrote a great number of books and plays. And many of his stories were about the people he met on his travels all over the world.

Maugham became a rich man. Eighty million copies of his books were sold while he was alive.

Somerset Maugham died in Cap Ferrat, France on 16 December 1965. He was 91 years old.

FOOTPRINTS IN THE JUNGLE

1

The Death of Bronson

In my travels round the world, I have stayed in many strange and interesting places. One of the places I like best is Malaya. Malaya is a beautiful place. It is also a place where I have heard the strangest stories.

Once I was staying in a town in Malaya called Tanah Merah. It used to be a port, and it has a small, beautiful harbour and a long sandy beach on both sides of the harbour. When I was in Tanah Merah, I stayed with a man called Gaze. Gaze was the chief policeman in the district. And I was sure that he would tell me some strange stories.

I was not wrong. On my first evening in Tanah Merah, I went down with Gaze to the British Club[1]. We had a drink and played cards with a married couple, Mr and Mrs Cartwright. Mr Cartwright was a very quiet and ordinary man but Mrs Cartwright seemed to be a very intelligent and determined[2] woman. I did not think that they were in any way unusual.

I went back with Gaze to his villa and we had a pleasant meal. Gaze was rather quiet at first but, as we sat outside on the verandah after the meal, he started to talk. He asked me a question and it really surprised me.

'If I told you that you were sitting with a murderer this evening,' Gaze asked me, 'would you believe me?'

'I don't think I would,' I replied with surprise in my voice.

'Well, let me tell you a story,' continued Gaze. 'After I have told you the story, perhaps you will believe me.'

We had a drink and played cards with a married couple,
Mr and Mrs Cartwright.

This was what I had been hoping for. Gaze was going to tell me a story. I sat back in my seat with my coffee and a glass of brandy, and I waited for Gaze to begin.

'I first met Mrs Cartwright twenty years ago,' said Gaze. 'Her name then was not Cartwright. It was Bronson. She was married to a rubber planter[3] called Bronson.'

'You were not living here at that time?' I asked.

'No,' replied Gaze. 'We were living a long way from here – in the rubber-growing area. I was a policeman in a little town. Bronson was the manager of a rubber estate[3] five miles away. He and his wife lived in a house there.'

'What was Mrs Bronson like twenty years ago?' I asked. 'She was much thinner than she is now,' replied Gaze. 'She had a lot of dark hair and her blue eyes were very pretty. She did not look so determined as she does now.'

'What was Mr Bronson like?' I asked.

'He was a big man with a red face and red hair,' said Gaze. 'He liked sports and was very friendly. Everyone liked him.

'One day, the Bronsons brought a friend to the British Club in the town,' Gaze went on. 'His name was Cartwright. He had been a friend of Mr Bronson's at school. Cartwright was a rubber planter. Many rubber planters lost their jobs when the price of rubber fell[4]. Cartwright had lost his job and he had no money. Mrs Bronson told Cartwright that he could stay with them as long as he liked.'

Gaze took off his glasses to clean them.

'Bronson was murdered,' he said suddenly.

———

'I shall never forget that night,' continued Gaze, after a moment's silence. 'Mrs Bronson, Cartwright and I were in the club having a drink.'

7

'Where was Bronson?' I asked.

'He had gone to another town not far away. He was getting money from the bank to pay the workers on his estate. He cycled to this town on a path through the jungle. Then he was going to come to the club after he got the money.'

'But he didn't come?' I asked.

'No. We waited a long time,' said Gaze. 'Then a policeman came in and asked to speak to me alone. He told me that a white man had been found shot dead in the jungle. I knew at once that it was Bronson.'

'It must have been a shock for you all,' I said.

'Yes, it was terrible,' said Gaze. 'When I told Mrs Bronson, she burst into tears. Cartwright turned white. I sent them both home and went for the doctor. Then we walked with the policeman to the place in the jungle where Bronson was lying.'

'Wasn't it dark by then?' I asked.

'Yes, it was dark, but we had lamps with us. The three of us walked along the jungle path, first the policeman, then the doctor, then me. I knew that we were going to find Bronson's body, of course, and I was expecting a shock. But when we suddenly saw the body lying on the ground beside a bicycle, it was horrible.'

Gaze paused. We both sat for a moment listening to the sounds of the jungle around us. Then Gaze went on. 'I knew at once that it was Bronson. I could see his red hair clearly. But I knew that we would have to take a closer look. I have been a policeman for many years and I've seen many terrible things. But I always feel sick when I see a dead body. I was glad the doctor was there. The doctor could see by the light of the lamps that Bronson had been dead for several hours. He had been shot in the back of the head. He had died at once.'

'Bronson had been dead for several hours.'

'Did you notice anything else?' I asked.

'Yes. I saw the prints of his heavy boots in the sand on each side of the marks made by the bicycle wheels.'

'What did that tell you?' I asked.

'It told me that he had stopped the bicycle, perhaps to talk to someone. But I could see that he had put his feet on the ground. Then he had been shot from behind.'

'And what about the money he had with him?' I asked.

'The money was gone, of course,' said Gaze. 'And his watch was gone too. Bronson always carried a gold watch. Now it was gone.'

'Then there was no doubt about why he had been killed?' I said.

'No,' said Gaze. 'It was clear that he had been killed by a gang of robbers. I knew that it would be difficult to find them. Many people knew that Bronson always cycled along that path with the money from the bank.'

'What did you do?' I asked.

'I asked a lot of people a lot of questions,' replied Gaze. 'I spoke to all the people who knew Bronson. I asked them all where they had been and what they had been doing that day. Mrs Bronson and Cartwright had, of course, been at the British Club with me in the evening. Before that, Mrs Bronson had been at home and Cartwright had been out hunting in the jungle.'

'Who else knew that Bronson always cycled along that path?' I asked.

'All the workers on the rubber estate knew about it, of course. The workers knew that he went to collect their pay. I questioned them all, but they had all been at work all day. I found no one who could have murdered Bronson. So then I offered a reward of a thousand dollars to anyone who found the murderer. Then I sat down and waited.'

2

A Gold Watch and Money

Gaze paused. He gave me a cigar and took one for himself. I lit my cigar and sat back and waited. Gaze continued his story.

'I waited a whole year but my plan didn't work. No one came for the thousand dollars reward. I thought Bronson's murderer would never be found. Then a year after Bronson's death, I heard two surprising pieces of news.'

I said nothing, but waited for Gaze to tell me about the two pieces of news.

'Firstly,' said Gaze, 'Cartwright and Mrs Bronson had got married. It was a surprise, but when I thought about it, I realised it was very natural. Cartwright had helped Mrs Bronson at a difficult time. He must have felt very sorry for her. She was lonely and needed someone to look after her.'

'Were they still living on the rubber estate where Bronson had been manager?' I asked.

'No,' replied Gaze. 'Cartwright had been given a job as manager of another rubber estate. The rubber estate which they live on now.'

'What was the other piece of news?' I asked.

'We caught a Chinaman with Bronson's watch. He was trying to sell the watch,' said Gaze.

I remembered at once that it was not just Bronson's money that had been stolen. His watch had been taken as well. But I did not understand how Gaze had caught the Chinaman.

Gaze went on to explain what had happened.

'Mrs Bronson had described the watch to me, and I had told my policemen to look out for it. The Chinaman had tried to sell the watch to a man on the street. By chance, this man had heard about the watch, and immediately told

11

a policeman. The Chinaman was arrested and brought to my office.'

Gaze smiled grimly at me.

'I was very, very glad to see him,' he continued. 'I had not heard anything about the Bronson case for over a year. When this poor Chinaman was brought to me, I was sure that at last I was going to find Bronson's murderer.'

'And what could this Chinaman tell you?' I asked excitedly.

'First I asked him where he had got the watch,' said Gaze. 'The Chinaman said that he had bought it from a man. But he did not know this man's name. I did not believe him. I told the Chinaman about the murder of Bronson, and said that he could be accused of murder. The poor man was very frightened. Then he said that he had found the watch.'

'He found it!' I said. 'Where?'

'His answer surprised me,' said Gaze. 'He said that he had found it in the jungle. I asked him when he had found it. He said he had found it a few days before. I asked to see the watch. The Chinaman quickly pulled it out of his pocket and laid it on my desk. I took the watch and tried to open it. This was difficult. When I finally opened it, I could see why it was so difficult. The inside of the watch was covered with rust. At once I knew the Chinaman's story was true. This watch had been lying in the jungle for a year.'

'What did you do next?' I asked.

'I told the Chinaman to take me to the exact place where he had found the watch,' Gaze continued. 'He was so afraid that he agreed immediately. We drove to the edge of the jungle with three of my policemen. Then we walked along the jungle path.'

'Where did he take you?' I asked.

'To the exact place where Bronson was killed,' Gaze replied. 'The Chinaman said that he had found the watch just a few yards from the path. The watch had been lying between two large stones.'

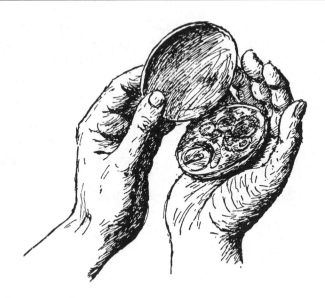

Gaze paused.

'I didn't understand that,' he said.

'Why not?' I asked.

'Well,' explained Gaze, 'if Bronson was killed by robbers, why did the robbers not keep the watch? The watch was made of gold, you know.'

'I see what you mean,' I said.

'Somebody had put the watch there to hide it,' said Gaze, looking at me closely.

'What would you have thought then?' he asked me.

'I don't know,' I answered.

'Well,' said Gaze, 'I'll tell you what I thought. If someone had tried to hide the watch, then the money might be hidden there as well. So I decided to search for the money.'

'In the jungle?' I asked. 'How could you hope to find the money in the jungle?'

'I knew that there was very little hope of finding such a small thing as a wallet in the jungle,' said Gaze. 'Still, we tried. There were five of us, the three policemen, the Chinaman and myself. We searched the area where the Chinaman had found the watch. We searched with great care, and it was very hard work. After several hours, I was hot, thirsty and angry. I decided that it was foolish to look for the money any longer. Suddenly, the Chinaman gave a cry. He had found an old, dirty wallet under the roots of a tree. And in the wallet were a lot of banknotes and some papers with the name "Bronson" on them.'

'So Bronson was not killed by a gang of robbers,' I remarked.

'No,' replied Gaze. 'Bronson's murderer had not taken his money.'

3

Mr and Mrs Cartwright

I remembered how Gaze had started his story. He had told me that we had been playing cards with a murderer. But there were several things I still did not understand.

'How did you discover . . .?'

Gaze smiled. I did not complete my question. He knew what I was going to ask.

'The footprints in the jungle,' said Gaze. 'I remembered the footprints made by Bronson's boots in the sand of the path.'

'Ah, yes,' I said. 'You said that Bronson must have stopped to talk to someone.'

'Exactly,' said Gaze. 'And it must have been someone that Bronson knew quite well, because the prints were deep. He had stood there for several minutes.'

Although I knew what Gaze was going to say next, it still came as a shock.

'Cartwright killed Bronson.'

Gaze went on to explain.

'Cartwright had been out hunting. He had a gun with him, and he knew that Bronson would be coming along that track on his bicycle. Cartwright stopped Bronson and talked with him for a few minutes. Then, as Bronson started to cycle off, Cartwright shot him in the back of the head. He hid the money and the watch in the jungle. He wanted people to think that Bronson had been murdered by a gang of robbers.'

'There is still one thing that I cannot understand,' I said. 'Why did Cartwright kill the man who had helped him?'

'Cartwright was in love with Mrs Bronson,' said Gaze simply. 'And she loved him. She made him do it.'

'But could they not just have run away together?' I asked.

'No,' Gaze answered. 'Where could they run to? No one in Malaya would help a man who had stolen his friend's wife. And Bronson had all the money. Cartwright and Mrs Bronson had no money. They had to kill him.'

'But what did you do about it?' I asked.

'Nothing,' said Gaze. 'Absolutely nothing.'

'But why not?' I asked.

'What could I do?' returned Gaze. 'I could prove nothing.'

'You found the watch and the money,' I said.

'A robber might have hidden them there. Perhaps the robber was afraid to come back and pick them up later,' said Gaze.

'What about the footprints?' I asked.

'Bronson might have stopped to light a cigarette. Or, there may have been something lying across the path which made him stop. No, I could prove nothing. I did nothing, and the Bronson murder was forgotten.'

'So these murderers are free today!' I said.

'You played cards with them this evening,' said Gaze, with a smile.

'But you are a policeman!' I cried. 'Surely it is your job to arrest murderers?'

'A policeman's job is to stop crime,' replied Gaze calmly, 'and to catch people who break the law. But any man can do something he knows is wrong when he cannot see any other thing to do. In my opinion, the important thing is not what people do, but what they are.'

I thought of the quiet old gentleman and his white-haired wife with whom we had played cards. I found it difficult to think of them as murderers.

'Do you never feel uncomfortable when you are with them?' I asked. 'They cannot be very nice people.'

'You are wrong,' said Gaze. 'They are about the nicest people I know here.'

'It must be terrible for the Cartwrights to live with the memory of the murder,' I said.

'A man's memory is a strange thing,' said Gaze. 'I think that a man can forget about something he has done. He can even forget something as terrible as a murder if he is certain that he will never be found out.'

THE TAIPAN

1

The Taipan's Discovery

The Taipan was an Englishman. He had come to China when he was a young man and had lived there for thirty years. At that time he worked as a clerk for a big English company. He worked very hard and, as the years went by, he was given more and more important jobs in the company. Now he was number one in the company's second largest office in China. He had become a very important man. The Chinese called him 'Taipan' – the Chinese word for 'Great Man'.

The Taipan was also very rich. He lived in a large house at the edge of the town. This house was built of white stone and it had wide verandahs. He lived here with his three servants and he had his office in the house, too.

One warm afternoon, the Taipan was walking back to his large house. He had been to lunch with the manager of the bank in the town and had had a lot to eat and drink. As he walked, he thought of his life in China.

'I live very well,' said the Taipan to himself. 'That was an excellent meal at the bank. It was almost as good as the meals that I have at home.'

The Taipan smiled to himself. He liked his food and since he had become a rich man in China, he ate very well. He had not eaten such good food all his life. He remembered his childhood in England.

I didn't eat so well when I was a boy in England, thought the Taipan. What a good thing I came to China! Now I'm rich and important. I am the Taipan! If I had stayed in England, I would still be a poor clerk.

The Taipan thought of his family in England. His parents were not rich. His father had been a clerk and his brothers were clerks. Even his sisters were married to clerks.

They must be pleased with the presents I send them every year at Christmas time, thought the Taipan. They're not rich enough to buy silk or expensive tea. But I'm rich enough to buy these expensive things and to send them to my family. And that's because I came to China all those years ago, and because I have worked very hard. I'll never go back to England.

The Taipan was pleased with himself and he was pleased with his life in China. It was a beautiful day and as he walked along on his way home, he came to the town cemetery. He liked to walk through this cemetery because it was so clean and tidy.

Some of the people buried in the cemetery were Englishmen. There were some sailors who had been drowned in a storm. And there were also some young men whom the Taipan had known. They had come to China, like the Taipan, to work as clerks for companies. Some of them had fallen ill and died and others had died from drinking too much. The Taipan stopped beside one grave. A man lay there who had worked for the same company as the Taipan. He had been a very clever man. If he had lived, he would have been Taipan now.

The Taipan felt some pleasure as he looked at these graves. He was stronger than the men who lay there. He smiled as he thought of these poor, dead people. He had beaten them. He had lived longer than them. And now he was the Taipan.

The Taipan continued his walk through the cemetery. Suddenly he saw two Chinamen digging a grave. This surprised him because he did not know that anyone in the town had died recently. He always knew about these things. He was an important man and he always heard about everything that happened in the town. But this grave was a mystery.

Suddenly he saw two Chinamen digging a grave.

'Who is that grave for?' the Taipan asked the workmen.

The two Chinese workmen did not stop digging the grave. They did not even look up from the deep hole. They continued to throw up heavy lumps of earth with their spades.

'Whose grave is that?' asked the Taipan again.

The Taipan had been in China for thirty years, but had never learned to speak Chinese. These two Chinese workmen did not understand the Taipan's question.

'Tell me whose grave that is!' he started again. One of the workmen answered him in Chinese. The Taipan did not understand what he had said.

'Fools!' cried the Taipan. 'Why can't you speak English?'

The Chinese workmen went on digging. The Taipan saw that he could not get an answer and so he left them and walked on towards his house.

But the Taipan was worried. Whose grave were the two men digging? No one in the town had died. A woman had a sick child but he had not heard that the child had died. And this grave was too big for a child. It was a grave for a man, and a big man too.

The Taipan did not like things which he did not understand. He decided to find out whose grave it was.

2

The Taipan is Worried

When the Taipan arrived back at his house, he went straight into his office. Immediately he asked one of his Chinese clerks to come into his office.

'Who has died recently in the town?' he asked the clerk.

'No one, sir,' replied the clerk.

'Go to the cemetery and talk to the workmen who are digging

a grave there,' ordered the Taipan. 'I want to know who that grave is for.'

'Yes, sir,' said the clerk, and he left the office.

The Taipan began to work at some papers. He tried to stop worrying about the mysterious grave. Soon the clerk returned to the Taipan's office.

'Well, did you find out about the grave?' asked the Taipan.

'No, sir,' replied the clerk. 'The workmen you told me about were gone. There was no one in the cemetery to ask.'

Now the Taipan began to get angry. He decided to speak to his chief servant, who always knew what was happening in the town.

'Do you know of anyone who has recently died in the town?'

'No, sir,' replied the servant. 'I have not heard of any death in the town.'

I knew no one was dead, said the Taipan to himself. But what is that grave for? Then he spoke aloud to his servant.

'Go at once to the overseer[5] of the cemetery and ask him why these workmen are digging a grave when no one has died.'

As the servant was leaving the room, the Taipan added, 'Let me have a glass of whisky before you go.'

The Taipan did not know why the grave made him so uncomfortable and he tried to forget it. When he had drunk the whisky, he felt better and he was able to finish his work.

He thought of his plans for the evening. He would go down to the British Club in the town and play cards. The Taipan enjoyed playing cards. He would play cards until it was time for dinner. This thought helped him to forget the grave.

Then his servant returned with the overseer of the cemetery.

'Why were two men digging a grave in the cemetery today?' the Taipan asked immediately. 'Nobody is dead.'

The overseer's reply was a shock for the Taipan.

'There is no new grave in the cemetery,' he said.

'What do you mean?' cried the Taipan angrily. 'There were two workmen digging a grave in the cemetery this afternoon.'

The cemetery overseer and the Taipan's servant looked at one another.

'We have just been to the cemetery together,' said the servant. 'There is no new grave there.'

The Taipan was about to say that he had seen the grave with his own eyes, but he stopped himself. He did not want the overseer or his own servant to think that he was mad. But the Taipan grew very red in the face with anger.

The two Chinamen stood looking at the Taipan. They said nothing. Their eyes did not move.

'All right. Get out,' said the Taipan. He could not say any more. The overseer and the servant looked at one another again and went out of the Taipan's office.

Just a few minutes after the overseer and the servant had left his office, the Taipan shouted for his servant again.

'Bring me some more whisky!' he cried.

Now the Taipan began to feel really uncomfortable and he started to sweat. He wiped his face with a handkerchief. His hands shook as he lifted his glass to his lips.

I saw that grave, he said to himself. I saw it, and I heard the lumps of earth hitting the ground as the workmen threw them up from the hole. And now my servant and the overseer say there is no new grave! What can it mean?

3

A Game of Cards

The Taipan felt uncomfortable, but he did not allow himself to worry over such a little thing.

If there is no grave, he said to himself, then I must have imagined it. People often imagine that they can see things which are not there. It happens when they are tired. That's it – I must be tired. I've been working too hard. I must see the doctor.

The Taipan felt better now. He had decided what was wrong and he had decided what he would do about it. He would go down to the British Club. The doctor was always there in the evening before dinner. He would ask the doctor to help him.

When he arrived at the club, the Taipan looked round. He knew all the men who were there. The Taipan walked over to a table and sat down. Many of the men in the club smiled and said, 'Good evening.'

The Taipan asked for a drink from one of the waiters. While the waiter was bringing his drink, the Taipan looked round at the other men in the club.

They were Englishmen, like the Taipan and they worked in the same Chinese town as him. Like him, they had been in China for many years. The Taipan knew almost everything about them.

He knew what they did every day. They worked in offices during the day and came to the club every evening.

The Taipan felt comfortable with these men around him. He was happy with the life which he and the other Englishmen had in China.

We live better here in China than we would if we were in England, he thought.

The three men that he always played cards with came over to his table. They sat down and began to play. But today something strange happened. The Taipan could not think properly. While he was playing cards, his thoughts returned again and again to the cemetery and the mysterious grave. He played cards very badly because he was thinking about what he had seen in the afternoon.

'I'm sorry,' said the Taipan to the three men. 'I can't play cards with you any more today.'

The three men were surprised. They knew that the Taipan enjoyed playing cards and it was strange that he had stopped suddenly.

'Aren't you feeling well?' one of the men asked the Taipan.

'No – I mean – yes. That is, excuse me,' he replied nervously. He did not know what to tell these men. He could not tell them about the grave he had seen. These men would think that he was mad. He left the table and started walking quickly towards the door. All the men in the club looked at him. They were surprised to see the Taipan acting so strangely.

As he was leaving, the Taipan saw the doctor sitting in a chair by the door. He was reading a newspaper. The Taipan remembered that he wanted to speak to the doctor. He wanted to tell the doctor about the grave he had seen. The Taipan stopped.

What will the doctor say? thought the Taipan. He may say that I am tired. He may say that I need a rest, because I have been working too hard. But he may not believe that I really saw the grave. He may think that I am mad!

The Taipan was afraid of what the doctor might say. He walked quickly past him and out of the club, without speaking to anyone.

4

The Taipan's Last Letter

Outside the British Club, the Taipan felt better. The fresh air helped him to think. He decided to go to the cemetery. He would see if the grave was there or not. That would end the mystery.

The Taipan walked quickly to the cemetery.

I shall be very angry with the overseer of the cemetery if I find that grave, thought the Taipan as he walked along. I don't like people who tell me lies.

When he reached the cemetery, he tried to open the gate, but it was locked. The Taipan became very angry. He went quickly to the overseer's house which was not far from the cemetery gate. He knocked on the door and the overseer's wife answered.

'Where is the overseer?' asked the Taipan at once. 'I must get into the cemetery, but the gate is locked.'

'He has gone out,' said the overseer's wife simply.

'Do you have the key to the gate?' asked the Taipan.

'No,' she replied, 'I'm afraid that my husband has taken it with him.'

The Taipan walked slowly away from the overseer's house. He felt very, very tired. He felt that he could do no more.

I must go home and lie down, thought the Taipan. He walked slowly back to his house. When he arrived home, he lay down to rest until it was time for dinner.

That evening, the Taipan sat down to eat alone. His servants brought him an excellent meal and he began to feel a little better again. The wine which he drank with the meal helped him to feel better.

After dinner, he drank a glass or two of brandy, then he went to bed. He fell at once into a very deep sleep.

Suddenly, in the middle of the night, the Taipan awoke. He sat up in his bed. His face was wet with sweat and his hands were shaking. He had been dreaming of the grave. He could see the Chinese workmen digging the grave with their spades. Now he knew why that grave and those workmen made him so afraid. It was *his* grave they were digging!

'No!' cried the Taipan in fear. 'I will not die in China! I hate China! The Chinese hate me! They have dug my grave, and now they are just waiting for me to die. They are waiting to bury me in it.

'I hate China!' he cried out again. 'I hate this town! I hate all the people in it! That overseer at the cemetery – he's just waiting for me to die! And my servant – he'll be happy when I'm dead. And all those stupid men at the British Club – they'll smile when they hear that I am in my grave. I hate them all!'

The Taipan went quickly to his office, lit the lamp and sat down at his desk. He took a piece of paper and began writing. He wrote a letter to the head office of his company in London. In this letter, he said that he was very ill and that he was returning to England at once.

The Taipan's servant found the letter the next morning. The Taipan was lying on his back on the floor beside his desk, holding the letter tightly in his hand. The Taipan was dead.

GIULIA LAZZARI

1

Ashenden Gets a Telegram

In 1915, during the First World War, I was working for the British Secret Service[6] in Switzerland. Switzerland was not fighting in the war and I could work there in safety. My job was to collect information from British spies[7] in Germany and send this information to London.

I was staying at a very comfortable hotel in Geneva. My job did not keep me very busy, but I was never bored. Some days, I went rowing in a boat on Lake Geneva. Other days, I went riding outside the town. But sometimes, I just walked in the streets of the old city of Geneva. If the weather was bad, I stayed in my hotel room and read.

I like to meet people and talk to them. I was now working for the British Secret Service, but that was only a wartime job. I was really a writer. And to be a good writer, I needed to know a lot of people. But here in Switzerland, I had to be careful.

The German Secret Service also had agents[8] in Geneva. Perhaps one of them was staying in the same hotel as me. I did not want anyone to know that I was an agent. If that happened, I would have to leave this pleasant life in Geneva and return to London. Also, my life might be in danger. The German agents might try to kill me.

One afternoon, when I came back from a walk, the hotel porter gave me a telegram.

COME AT ONCE TO PARIS. AUNT MAGGIE IS VERY
ILL. STAYING AT HOTEL LOTTI. R.

This was a message from my chief in the British Secret Service.
He always called himself 'R'. I did not know his real name.

I did not have an aunt called Maggie. This was a secret
message. I was to go to Paris immediately and meet R in the
Hotel Lotti.

The express train for Paris left at eight o'clock in the evening.
I went up to my room and packed my bag. At a quarter to eight, I
left the hotel and walked to the railway station. I was happy that I
was going to Paris. I liked to travel by train, especially at night.

I got onto the train and found a sleeping-compartment. Soon
after the train started, I climbed into bed and fell asleep. A noise
woke me in the night and I lay awake for a long time, smoking a
cigarette. I liked being all alone in a little room on a train rushing
through the night. The sound of the wheels on the rails helped me
to think.

I'll be in Paris tomorrow morning, I thought. And I'll find out
why R sent me that strange telegram.

2

Chandra Lal

W hen the train arrived in Paris the next morning, I got off
and telephoned R's office.

'How is Aunt Maggie?' I asked when R answered the
telephone.

'I'm glad that you've come so quickly,' replied R. 'Aunt
Maggie is very ill, but it will do her good to see you.'

29

Agents had to be careful when they were speaking to one another on the telephone. They always spoke secretly. 'When would Aunt Maggie like to see me?' I asked.

'As soon as possible,' R replied.

'All right,' I said. 'I'll be at the Hotel Lotti in half an hour.'

Thirty minutes later, I arrived at the Hotel Lotti. A man in British army uniform took me up to R's room. R was busy writing at a desk covered with papers.

'Sit down,' said R. 'You'll have to wait a few minutes. I must finish this writing.'

I had time to have a long look at R. He looked older than the last time I had seen him. There were more lines in his face and his hair was greyer. R worked very hard. He was up at seven o'clock every morning and he worked until late at night.

Before he had started working for the Secret Service, R had been a soldier in India and Jamaica. Now he was an important officer in the Secret Service because he was clever, brave and determined. But he could also be a cruel man. He did not care what happened to anyone who opposed him.

At last R put his pen down. He looked at me over the desk.

'You've been doing a good job in Geneva,' he said, without smiling.

'Thank you, sir,' I replied.

R's face suddenly became cold and hard.

'Have you ever heard of a man called Chandra Lal?' R asked.

'No, sir,' I said.

R took a photograph out of a drawer in his desk and handed it to me.

'That's Chandra Lal,' he said.

It was a photograph of an Indian. I had never seen him before. The Indian was fat and had a dark face with thick black hair and brown eyes. He was wearing European clothes.

'Here's another photograph,' said R.

This second photograph showed Chandra Lal as a young man.

He was not so fat and, this time, he was wearing Indian clothes.

'What do you think of him?' asked R.

'He looks strong and determined,' I replied.

'I'll tell you all we know about him,' said R.

I sat back in my chair and listened.

'Chandra Lal is one of the Indians who are against British rule in India,' R began. 'As a young man, he worked as a lawyer. Then he became interested in politics. He is a very good talker and he can persuade people to believe him and do as he wants. He believes that the British should be forced to leave India. And he is ready to use any way possible.'

I understood why the Secret Service was interested in this man.

'Chandra Lal was arrested once,' R continued. 'He had persuaded a lot of people in an Indian town to start

fighting in the streets. Two people were killed and many more were hurt.'

I looked down at the photographs of Chandra Lal. R was right. This man was strong – and dangerous.

'After that, Chandra was in prison in India for two years,' R went on. 'But he was free again in 1914 when the war started. And since then, he has been a problem.' R leaned forward and his face became even harder.

'The Germans gave him a lot of money and asked him to start trouble in India. And they were successful. Many British soldiers could not come back to fight in Europe. They had to be left in India. They were needed there to stop the trouble that Chandra Lal was causing.

'Chandra Lal used the money from the Germans to buy bombs and guns,' said R. 'There was a lot of trouble and many more people were killed. At last, the police offered a reward for his capture.'

'But he wasn't caught?' I asked.

'No, he escaped from India to America. Then he went to Sweden, and from Sweden to Germany. Finally, he left Germany and went to Lausanne in Switzerland.'

'But he cannot cause us trouble in Switzerland,' I said.

'This man is dangerous in any place,' replied R. 'He is clever and brave. And he works very hard. With money and help from the Germans, Chandra Lal can cause a lot of trouble. We must catch him.'

'But not while he's in Switzerland,' I interrupted. 'Switzerland is a neutral[9] country. We have no power there.'

'That's true,' replied R. 'We cannot get him in Switzerland. But there *is* a way of catching him.'

I leaned forward. This was going to be the most interesting part of R's story. But R's next words came as a complete surprise to me.

'Chandra Lal has fallen in love,' he said.

3

Giulia Lazzari

R reached again into his desk drawer and brought out some papers. He handed them to me.

'Here are some of Chandra Lal's love-letters.'

I took the letters and began to look through them, but R stopped me.

'Don't read them now. Take them with you and read them later.'

'What can you tell me about the woman?' I asked.

R took another photograph out of his desk drawer. It was a photograph of a woman. She was dressed in the kind of clothes that are worn by Spanish dancers. She was a tall woman with long black hair. I did not think that the woman was pretty, but perhaps many men would find her attractive.

'Her name is Giulia Lazzari,' said R. 'She's a dancer. She was born in Italy, but she does Spanish dancing. She has danced in clubs and small theatres all over Europe for the last ten years.'

'How did Chandra Lal meet her?' I asked.

'She was dancing in a small theatre in Berlin,' replied R. 'Chandra Lal was there one evening. He fell in love with her immediately. He met her in her room behind the stage after she had finished dancing.'

'They seem a strange pair,' I said.

'They are a strange pair – an Italian woman who does Spanish dancing and an Indian lawyer who is paid by the Germans. But then, love is a strange thing.'

I smiled at R's remark.

'Where is Giulia Lazzari now?' I asked. And again R's reply was surprising.

'She's in the women's prison at Holloway in London.'

'In prison?' I asked.

'She was arrested two weeks ago for spying.'

'How did you discover her?'

'Giulia Lazzari arrived in England six weeks ago,' replied R. 'She had arranged to dance in London and in several other towns.'

'But that does not seem unusual,' I said.

'No. But she had been in Germany recently and we watch people who have come from Germany very carefully. We soon learnt that she was sending letters to Switzerland and getting replies in English.'

'There's nothing wrong with that, either,' I interrupted.

'No,' agreed R, 'but we opened two of the letters to see what was in them. And what we learnt was very interesting. Giulia Lazzari was writing her letters to Chandra Lal.'

'How did you discover that?'

'Chandra Lal sent a photograph of himself in one of the letters.'

'That was a foolish thing to do,' I said.

'Yes, it was foolish,' agreed R. 'Especially for such a clever man as Chandra Lal. But Giulia Lazzari had asked him for a photograph. He was so much in love with her that he could not refuse.'

'You said that you opened two letters,' I said. 'What was in the other one?'

'A promise to give information to Chandra Lal,' replied R.

'But how was she going to get this information out of England?'

'She wasn't even going to try,' said R. 'Giulia Lazzari had written all the information down in notebooks and she was keeping the notebooks in her bags. Her idea was to leave England and meet Chandra Lal somewhere, perhaps in Switzerland. Then she could give him the notebooks.'

'And then Chandra Lal could pass the information to the Germans?'

'Yes, that was the plan.'

'What happened after Giulia Lazzari went into Holloway prison?' I asked.

'Nothing,' R replied. 'I left her alone for a week. I knew that prison would frighten her. Holloway prison is not a very cheerful place, you know.'

'No prison is a cheerful place,' I remarked.

'I left her alone for a week and then I went to see her. She was very unhappy and afraid. And I made her even more afraid.

'I told her that she could be kept in prison for ten years for spying,' went on R. 'Then I told her that I could get her out of prison. But she had to agree to help us. At first she would not tell me anything. She said that she had never collected information. But I told her that we had found her notebooks.'

'What did she do then?' I asked.

'One week in Holloway prison had been enough,' replied R. 'The thought of another ten years there frightened her. She started to cry and she told me everything. But I also wanted her to help me in another way. I had to get her to agree to my plan.'

'Your plan?' I asked.

'Yes, I have a very simple plan,' replied R. 'Giulia Lazzari is going to write another letter to Chandra Lal. She is going to ask him in this letter to leave Switzerland and meet her in France. When he is in France, we can arrest him. Then Giulia Lazzari can go free. We'll give her a ticket to Spain or to South America.'

'But Giulia Lazzari is in love with Chandra Lal,' I said. 'She'll never agree to help the British Secret Service.'

'You're wrong there,' replied R. 'My plan will work for two reasons.'

'What are they?' I asked.

'Firstly, Giulia Lazzari does not want to stay in Holloway prison for ten years. And secondly, Chandra Lal is madly in love with her. He is sure to come to France to see her. And there's a third reason.'

'What's that?'

'I'm sending one of my best men with Giulia Lazzari to see that my plan works.'

'Who?' I asked.

'You,' replied R simply.

4

On the Train to Thonon

Two days later, I was again standing in a railway station in Paris. It was eight o'clock in the evening and I was watching people getting onto a train. This train was leaving soon for the town of Thonon in the east of France. Thonon is in France, on one side of Lake Geneva, and Switzerland is on the other side of the lake.

It was getting late and there was only a short time before the train left. Then I saw the three people I was looking for – two men and one woman. They were rather far away from me and I could not see the woman clearly. But I remembered the photograph in R's office. And I was sure that this was the same woman.

I picked up my bag and walked quickly behind them. When the three people got into a carriage, I climbed onto the train. I found my sleeping-compartment and put my bag down. A few moments later, the train started on its journey to Thonon.

Firstly, I thought to myself, I must make sure that this woman is really Giulia Lazzari.

I walked down the train. I saw the woman sitting in the corner of a compartment. I could only see part of her face, but I recognised her immediately. It was Giulia Lazzari. There was a man sitting opposite her. Suddenly someone touched my arm. I looked round quickly and saw a man standing beside me. It was the other man who had been in the station with Giulia Lazzari.

'Hello, sir,' said the man. 'We've brought the woman with us to France. I think you're waiting to meet her. R told us that you would get on the train in Paris.'

'Good,' I replied. 'You and your friend wait outside. I'll talk to the lady now.'

The man nodded. He opened the compartment door and

spoke to the other man. Both men came out and I went in. Giulia Lazzari looked up as I came into the compartment. She looked tired and very frightened.

I smiled at her, but she looked at me angrily.

'I hope you're having a pleasant journey,' I said.

Giulia Lazzari did not reply. I looked at her more closely. She was no longer young – about thirty-five years old. And she was not smartly dressed. She wore a little hat which hid her long black hair. The only beautiful thing about her was her eyes. She stared at me as I sat down opposite her.

'A cigarette?' I said.

She did not reply, but took a cigarette from my case. I lit the cigarette for her. She looked at me for a long time while she started to smoke. Then she blew out a cloud of smoke.

'Who are you?' she asked.

'My name is not important,' I replied. 'The important thing is that you are going to Thonon and I'm going with you.'

Giulia Lazzari looked at me with frightened eyes.

'What are you going to do with me in Thonon?' she asked.

'I've got a room for you there in the Hotel de la Place. You'll be very comfortable.'

'So you're my guard,' said Giulia Lazzari sadly. 'I'm still in prison.'

'No, you're no longer in prison and I'm not your guard. I'm here to look after you.'

'You *are* my guard, then,' said Giulia Lazzari unhappily.

'If you say so,' I replied. 'Now I have something important to tell you. I have a railway ticket in my pocket. It's a ticket from Thonon to Spain.'

'You're going to set me free?' She looked as if she could not believe what she had heard. But her eyes quickly grew dark again.

'What do I have to do before you will give me that ticket?' she asked.

'You're right. There is something that we want you to do.

38

Giulia Lazzari looked at me for a long time.

And, after you do it, we will set you free.'

'What do you want me to do?' she asked.

'You must write a letter to your friend, Chandra Lal. You must ask him to come to meet you in France.'

'So that's your plan!' she cried. 'I'll never write such a letter. I'll never ask Chandra Lal to come to France. He would never come to France, anyway. He knows that it's much too dangerous for him in France.'

'If you do not write the letter, you will be taken back to England,' I told her calmly. 'And you will be put in Holloway prison for ten years.'

Giulia Lazzari began to cry.

'It's terrible,' she said through her tears. 'You are very cruel men. But I can't go back to that terrible prison again. And for ten years! What will I look like in ten years' time?'

I did not reply. Giulia Lazzari was even more afraid of going to prison than of losing her Indian lover. I began to think that R's plan might work after all.

5

The Letter

After a few moments, Giulia Lazzari stopped crying and looked up at me.

'What do you want me to write?' she asked.

I felt pleased. I had been right. R's plan was going to work.

'Tell Chandra Lal about the information which you have collected in England,' I said. 'Say that if he wants to see you, he must come to Thonon.'

Giulia Lazzari was a little calmer now. She thought for a moment.

'But he'll tell me to come to Switzerland,' she said. 'He knows that he can be arrested by the British in France. I must give him a reason why I can't come to Switzerland.'

I had already thought of a reason.

'Tell Chandra Lal that there is something wrong with your passport and you can't get into Switzerland. Also, tell him that you have chosen Thonon because it's so quiet here. Say that it's impossible to believe that there's a war going on.'

Giulia Lazzari looked hard at me across the compartment. There was hatred and anger in her eyes.

'You've thought out your plan carefully, haven't you?' she said.

I said nothing.

'I must do as you say,' said Giulia Lazzari. 'I don't want to go back to that prison. When do you want me to write the letter?'

'Now,' I replied. I stood up and opened the door of the compartment. One of the two British agents was standing outside.

'The lady wants to write a letter,' I told the man. 'Get some paper and an envelope.'

I went back to my seat opposite Giulia Lazzari and waited. She was sitting looking sadly out of the window. It was now getting dark and the lights went on in the compartment. It was difficult to see anything out of the window. Soon the man came back with some paper and an envelope. He went outside again and I gave the paper to Giulia Lazzari.

It was hard for her to write the letter. She hated what she was doing. She looked up at me again. But the thought of prison was too terrible for her. She wrote the letter exactly as I wanted it.

When she had finished writing, I took the letter and read it. She had written everything just as I had told her. I gave her back the letter.

'Write at the bottom that you love Chandra Lal very much,' I said. 'Tell him that you hope to see him soon.'

This letter had to be exactly like her other love-letters. If it was not exactly the same, Chandra Lal might think that there was something wrong.

When she had finished, I read the letter again carefully. I was satisfied now and put the letter in the envelope.

'Now write the address on the envelope,' I told her.

Giulia Lazzari wrote the address:

> *Chandra Lal,*
> *Hotel Royale,*
> *Lausanne,*
> *Switzerland*

Then I took the letter and left the compartment. The agent was still waiting outside. I gave him the letter and told him to post it at the next station. Then I returned to the compartment.

'Thank you for your help,' I said to Giulia Lazzari. 'Now, try to sleep for the rest of the journey. I'll see you again when we arrive at Thonon in the morning.'

Giulia Lazzari did not reply. She was still looking sadly out of the darkened window.

I left her and returned to my own compartment. I was feeling very tired. I went to bed and fell asleep at once.

When the train stopped in Thonon the next morning, I got out of the carriage. The two British agents were waiting for me with Giulia Lazzari.

'You can go now,' I told the men. 'The lady is coming with me.'

The two men walked away and I took Giulia Lazzari to a taxi. It was quite a long drive to the hotel, but neither of us spoke. I was sure that Giulia Lazzari was thinking hard about a way to escape from her terrible situation.

The Hotel de la Place was a small hotel in the corner of a quiet little square. The manager of the hotel showed us up to the room that had been prepared for Giulia Lazzari.

'It's a very nice room,' I told the manager. The manager thanked me and left us alone.

'I hope that you will be comfortable here,' I said, turning to Giulia Lazzari. 'Ask the manager for anything that you want. He knows nothing about you. You are a guest of the hotel. You are absolutely free.'

Giulia Lazzari looked at me quickly.

'Do you mean that I'm free to go out of the hotel?' she asked.

'Of course,' I replied.

'But with a policeman on either side, I suppose,' she said.

'Not at all,' I said. 'You can go out and come in freely. But you must promise to write no letters without telling me. And you mustn't leave Thonon until I give you permission.'

'I must agree to do everything you tell me,' she answered. 'If I don't, I'll be taken back to England and to prison. I promise that I won't write any letters and I won't try to leave Thonon.'

I thanked her and left the hotel. I took a taxi and drove to the police station. The chief of the police in Thonon was waiting for me.

'We are ready,' he told me. 'My best men are already waiting outside the hotel.'

I was satisfied now that nothing could go wrong. I went back to the taxi and drove to a little house just outside Thonon. This was where I was going to stay while in Thonon.

The long journey had made me feel tired and dirty. I had a bath and a shave. Then I sat down in a comfortable armchair and spent the rest of the day reading an exciting book.

6

Police Report

Later that evening, a dark little Frenchman came to visit me. The man had sharp eyes and was unshaven. He was wearing old and dirty clothes and he looked quite poor. I invited him in and gave him a glass of wine.

'My name's Felix,' said the visitor. 'I'm from the Thonon police. I've been watching the lady who came with you.'

'What has she been doing?' I asked.

'She's had a busy day,' replied Felix. 'She came out of the hotel about a quarter of an hour after you left. She was carrying some clothes and some jewels. She took these to a shop and sold them.'

'And what did she do then?'

'She went down to the quay where the boat sails between Lausanne and Thonon.'

'I thought that she would try that,' I said. 'The boat is the quickest and easiest way to get to Lausanne. She was hoping to get to Switzerland to meet Chandra Lal.'

'That's what she tried to do,' replied Felix. 'She bought a ticket for Lausanne and waited for the boat to come in.'

'Did she get on the boat?'

'No,' replied Felix. 'The passport officials[10] would not allow her to get on the boat. She had no passport.'

I knew that Giulia Lazzari had no passport. It was in my pocket.

'How did she explain the fact that she had no passport?' I asked Felix.

'She told the officials that she had lost it,' he replied.

'Did they believe her?'

'No,' replied Felix. 'They told her that she could not leave

France without a passport. In the end, she tried to give the official a hundred franc note to let her get on the boat.'

'She is not so clever as I thought,' I said when I heard that.

'No, it was a stupid thing to do,' agreed Felix. 'The passport official sent her away. He was very angry with her for trying to give him money. It's against the law.'

'Yes,' I agreed. 'A passport official won't let anyone through without a passport.'

Felix had nothing more to tell me. We had another glass of wine together and then Felix left me alone.

7

Another Letter

The following morning, I went to see Giulia Lazzari. At the hotel, the manager gave me a letter. It had been posted in Lausanne and it was addressed to Giulia Lazzari.

I took the letter up to her room. I knocked on the door and after some time she opened it. She was not happy to see me.

'Good morning,' I said cheerfully. 'Have you slept well?'

'No,' she replied angrily.

'I have a letter for you,' I told her, as I followed her into the room.

Her face changed at once.

'Give it to me,' she said.

I gave her the letter. When she had read it, she turned to me with a happy look on her face.

'He won't come,' she said with a laugh. 'You can't catch him. He's too clever for you.'

45

I took the letter and read it. It was a reply to the letter that Giulia Lazzari had written on the train. Chandra Lal said that he was very sad that Giulia Lazzari was not able to come to Lausanne.

'Please try to come here,' wrote Chandra Lal. 'I cannot come to France. It's too dangerous for me. I could be arrested by the French or the British Secret Service. I love you very much. It's terrible that we're so near each other and yet we can't meet. Try to get a new passport so that you can come to Switzerland.'

'He won't come,' said Giulia Lazzari with a laugh, when I had read the letter.

'You'll have to write another letter,' I told her simply. Giulia Lazzari stopped laughing immediately.

'Tell Chandra Lal that you cannot get a new passport,' I said. 'Tell him that the French officials refuse to give you one. Say that it is safe for him to come here to Thonon. Tell him that you would not ask him to come if there was any danger. Say that if he loves you, he will come to Thonon immediately.'

'No,' she cried. 'I won't do it.'

'Don't be a fool,' I told her. 'You know what will happen if you don't write this letter.'

Giulia Lazzari's face became very pale. There were tears in her eyes, but she stopped herself from crying.

'I won't do it,' she said in a determined voice.

'Very well,' I said and I stood up to leave.

'Yes – go. Go,' cried Giulia Lazzari suddenly. She threw herself on to the bed and started to cry.

'I'll be back,' I said.

As I went out, I locked the door behind me and put the key in my pocket. I went downstairs and made a telephone call. Then I went upstairs again, unlocked the door and went in. Giulia Lazzari was lying with her face on the bed. She was still crying.

I looked round the room. People think that travelling round the world as a dancer is an exciting life. But it is not true. I looked at Giulia Lazzari. Everything which she owned was in two small suitcases, lying in the corner. I would not like her life.

I wondered what sort of woman she really was. Who were her parents? What might she have been if she hadn't been a dancer? But I did not feel sorry for Giulia Lazzari. She had been persuaded to work as a spy against the British.

There was a knock at the door and the two men came in. When she saw them, Giulia Lazzari gave a cry of surprise and fear. They were the same British agents who had come with her from London.

'Why have you come here?' she asked.

'They've come to take you back to Holloway prison,' I told her.

'No. No – I won't go,' cried Giulia Lazzari and she threw herself back on the bed.

One of the two men went over to her and took her by the arm.

'Come along with us,' he said roughly.

'Don't touch me!' she cried angrily. 'Don't come near me!'

'You don't need to use force,' I told the men. 'She will come with you.'

The men stood back and Giulia Lazzari got up off the bed. She picked up her coat and her hat.

Is she brave enough to go back to London? I asked myself. Will she go to prison for ten years so that Chandra Lal can go free?

She put on her coat and hat and I nodded to one of the agents. The man stepped forward with a pair of handcuffs in his hand. When she saw the handcuffs, Giulia Lazzari jumped back and threw her arms in the air.

'No – no – not that,' she cried. 'I can't . . .'

She turned to me for help.

'Please stop them,' she cried. 'Stop them!'

'I can do nothing,' I told her.

She was crying again and she spoke through her tears.

'I'll do what you want. I'll write the letter.'

'No. No – I won't go,' cried Giulia Lazzari.

This was what I was waiting to hear. I made a sign to the two men and they left the room.

'You must give me time,' said Giulia Lazzari. 'I can't think clearly just now. You'll have to wait.'

'I can't wait,' I replied. 'You must write the letter now. You don't have to think. Just write down what I tell you.'

Giulia Lazzari sat down at a little table with her head between her hands. I placed paper and a pen in front of her. When she was ready, I started to tell her what to write.

'Dear Chandra Lal, I've had enough,' I began. I spoke slowly and Giulia Lazzari wrote down what I told her. 'I can't wait for you any longer. You don't love me very much, Chandra Lal, or you would come to see me. There is no danger here in Thonon. You are not very brave. I shall go back now to Paris. I loved you very much, but you didn't love me. It is finished. Goodbye, Giulia.'

I took the letter and read it through carefully. I knew Giulia Lazzari well now. I was able to write a letter that she might have written herself. Also, she had made some mistakes in the spelling. This made it look even more like one of her own letters.

'I'll leave you now,' I said, after Giulia Lazzari had written the address on the envelope. 'If this letter works, we'll catch Chandra Lal. Then I'll give you a ticket to Spain.'

Giulia Lazzari said nothing and I left her alone.

8

Chandra Lal Comes to Thonon

The following morning, I went down to the quay at Thonon with Felix, the policeman. There was a little wooden office on the quay. The passengers who came off the boat from Switzerland had to pass this office and show their passports at a window. A passport official sat at this window and Felix sat down beside him.

The two British agents were sitting in a waiting-room next to the passport office. If Chandra Lal came off the boat from Lausanne, Felix would tell the two men. Then they could come and arrest Chandra Lal.

I stood outside on the quay and watched the arrival of the boat from Lausanne. I felt excited.

Six passengers got off the boat and went past the passport office. None of them looked like an Indian.

'He hasn't come,' I said to Felix.

'No,' replied Felix. 'But there's a man with a letter.'

Felix pointed to a man on the other side of the passport office. He was one of the six passengers from the boat and he had a letter in his hand.

I went up to him.

'You have a letter,' I said to him. 'May I see it?'

The man looked frightened. He gave me the letter without saying a word. I looked at the address on the letter.

Madame Giulia Lazzari,
Hotel de la Place,
Thonon

It was Chandra Lal's handwriting. I thought quickly and then

I stood outside on the quay and watched the arrival of the boat from Lausanne.

gave the letter back to the man.

'Take this letter back,' I said. 'Give it to the person who sent it. Tell him that the lady is leaving for Paris today. She hasn't time to read the letter.'

The man nodded and went back on to the boat. A few minutes later, the boat left Thonon on its way back to Lausanne.

'When's the next boat?' I asked.

'At five o'clock in the evening,' replied Felix.

'Stay here with the two Englishmen,' I told him. 'I'll be back at five o'clock.'

I was a little late. When I got back to the quay a few minutes after five o'clock, the boat had already arrived. Felix came running to meet me.

'Quick!' he shouted. 'He's here.'

I started to run with Felix towards the passport office. We rushed into the waiting-room. A crowd of people were standing round a man who was lying on the floor.

'What has happened?' I asked.

'Look,' said Felix.

Chandra Lal was lying on the floor on his side. His eyes were open, but his body was still and he was dead.

'He killed himself,' said one of the British agents. 'He was too quick for us.'

I stared at the body.

'How did it happen?' I asked.

'There were only four passengers on the five o'clock boat,' replied Felix. 'The Indian was the last passenger to get off. When he showed his passport at the window, I asked him to come into the waiting-room for a moment. When he saw the two Englishmen, he knew immediately that he was caught.'

'Did he try to get away?' I asked.

'No,' replied Felix. 'He seemed to accept his capture quite calmly. He said that the waiting-room was too hot and he asked if he could take his coat off. I told him that he could. He took off

his coat and then turned to put it over a chair. Suddenly, he fell to the floor. He was dead before we could do anything.'

Felix bent down over the body and opened one of Chandra Lal's hands. There was a little bottle in the hand. Felix took it and gave it to me.

'Poison[11],' said Felix. 'He must have had the bottle of poison hidden in his hand. When he took his coat off and turned away from us, he was able to drink it. He had decided that it was better to die than to be caught by the British.'

'So we didn't catch Chandra Lal after all,' I said softly.

'Will your chief in London be angry?' asked Felix.

'I don't think so,' I replied. 'Chandra Lal will not cause us any more trouble. That's what my chief wanted. But I'm sorry that I wasn't here myself when Chandra Lal came off the boat.'

'I was surprised when you went away,' said Felix. 'Why didn't you wait here?'

'I was reading a very exciting book,' I told him. 'And I had left it at my house. I wanted to finish reading it.'

'But you work for the British Secret Service,' said Felix with a laugh. 'Isn't that exciting enough for you?'

9

The End

I left the quay and walked slowly back to the Hotel de la Place. It was the last time that I would have to go there and I was glad. I had begun to hate the hotel. It was a very sad place.

I knocked at the door of Giulia Lazzari's room and went in. She was sitting at the little table by the window, doing nothing. She looked up as I came in. When she saw my face, her own face changed.

'Something's happened?' she cried.

I said nothing. A look of fear came into Giulia Lazzari's face.

'He's caught,' she whispered.

'He's dead,' I said softly.

Giulia Lazzari did not cry and her reply surprised me.

'Dead,' she said simply. 'He had time to take the poison. Good. He escaped you after all.'

'What do you mean?' I asked. 'You knew about the poison. Why didn't you tell me?'

'Why should I tell you?' asked Giulia Lazzari. 'The poison was his last chance of escape. He always carried it with him. He was determined that the British would never catch him alive. I would never have told you about it.'

'Well, it doesn't matter now,' I said. 'Chandra Lal cannot trouble the British any longer, either in Europe or in India. You are free to go to Spain when you wish. Here's your ticket and your passport.'

I gave Giulia Lazzari an envelope and watched her as she opened it. I felt strange. I would never see her again. I did not even want to, but I did not hate her. I had studied this woman. And I had learnt a lot about her. I could write a letter that she might have written herself. But all that meant nothing now.

Giulia Lazzari had one more surprise for me. She stopped me as I was leaving the room.

'Wait,' she said. 'There's something you can do for me.'

'What's that? I asked.

'I gave Chandra Lal a present last year,' she replied. 'It was a watch and it cost me twelve pounds. Can I have it back?'

Points for Understanding

FOOTPRINTS IN THE JUNGLE

1

1 What surprising thing did Gaze tell Maugham about the Cartwrights?
2 Who was Mrs Cartwright married to when Gaze first knew her?
3 How did Gaze know that Bronson had stopped his bicycle before he was shot?
4 Why did Gaze think that Bronson had been killed by a gang of robbers?

2

1 What were the two surprising pieces of news that Gaze heard a year after Bronson's death?
2 The inside of Bronson's watch was covered with rust. What did this tell Gaze?
3 Why did Gaze decide that Bronson had not been killed by a gang of robbers?

3

1 Who murdered Bronson and why?
2 Why did Gaze not arrest the murderer?
3 Gaze was not able to prove anything. There were two other reasons why Bronson might have stopped his bicycle. What were they?

THE TAIPAN

1

1 Why was the Taipan pleased with his life in China?
2 Why did the Taipan feel some pleasure as he looked at the graves in the cemetery?
3 Why was the Taipan upset when he saw some workmen digging a grave?

2

1 What were the Taipan's plans for the evening?
2 Why did the Taipan feel really uncomfortable and start to sweat?

3

1 Why did the Taipan play cards so badly?
2 Why did the Taipan not speak to the doctor?

4

1 Did the Taipan really like his life in China?
2 Whose grave did the Taipan believe the workmen had been digging?

GIULIA LAZZARI

1

1 What was Ashenden's wartime job in Switzerland?
2 Who was Aunt Maggie and what was the meaning of the secret message?

2

1 Why was the British Secret Service interested in Chandra Lal?
2 Why could the British not arrest Chandra Lal in Switzerland?
3 What words of R's surprised Ashenden?

3

1 What was Giulia Lazzari's work?
2 Why had Chandra Lal been unable to refuse to send a photograph of himself to Giulia Lazzari?
3 What was R's plan?
4 R thought that his plan would succeed for three reasons. What were these three reasons?

4

1 Ashenden has a ticket in his pocket. Who was it for?
2 Why did Ashenden begin to think that R's plan might work?

5

1 Giulia Lazzari had to write three things in her letters to Chandra Lal.
    (a) She had something to give him – what?
    (b) She could not come herself to Switzerland – why?
    (c) She had chosen to come to Thonon – why?
2 Ashenden told Giulia Lazzari that she was allowed to go wherever she wished in Thonon. Was he telling the truth?

6

1 Who was Felix and what was his job?
2 Why did the passport officer not allow Giulia Lazzari to get on the boat for Switzerland?

7

1 Why did Chandra Lal refuse to come to France?
2 The British Secret Service knew that Chandra Lal loved Giulia Lazzari very much. How did Ashenden hope to use this fact in the second letter that he wanted Giulia Lazzari to write?
3 What finally persuaded Giulia Lazzari to write the second letter?

8

1 What did Ashenden tell the man who brought the letter for Giulia Lazzari?
2 How did Chandra Lal kill himself?
3 Why was Ashenden not at the quay when the boat arrived?

9

1 Why had Giulia Lazzari not told Ashenden about the poison?
2 What was the last surprise that Giulia Lazzari had for Ashenden?

Glossary

1 **British Club** (page 5)
  a building where people from Britain could meet together to drink and play cards etc.
2 **determined woman** (page 5)
  a woman who tries very hard to get what she wants.
3 **rubber planter/rubber estate** (page 7)
  a rubber estate is a forest where rubber trees are grown. The rubber is taken from the trees and sold to companies which make things like car tyres. A rubber planter is someone who works on a rubber estate. At the time of this story, most planters in the Far East were Englishmen.
4 **the price of rubber fell** (page 7)
  the world price of rubber changes from one year to the next. Where a rubber planter cannot get enough money for his rubber, he has great difficulties.
5 **overseer** (page 22)
  a person who is responsible for something. Chief or head person.
6 **British Secret Service** (page 28)
  an organisation which worked secretly to get information about enemy countries. At the time of this story, Britain and France were at war with Germany.
7 **spies** (page 28)
  people who worked for the Secret Service against the enemy.
8 **agents** (page 28)
  another word for spies.
9 **neutral** (page 32)
  a country which is not taking part in the fighting.
10 **passport official** (page 44)
  before crossing from France into Switzerland, Giulia Lazzari needed to have a passport. The passport official has the job of checking people's passports.
11 **poison** (page 53)
  something which kills a person when it is eaten or drunk.

W. SOMERSET MAUGHAM
unsimplified

FICTION

Liza of Lambeth
Mrs Craddock
The Magician
Of Human Bondage
The Moon and Sixpence
The Trembling of a Leaf
On a Chinese Screen
The Painted Veil
The Casuarina Tree
Ashenden
The Gentleman in the Parlour
Cakes and Ale
First Person Singular
The Narrow Corner

Ah King
Don Fernando
Cosmopolitans
Theatre
The Summing Up
Christmas Holiday
Books and You
The Mixture as Before
Up at the Villa
Strictly Personal
The Razor's Edge
Then and Now
Creatures of Circumstance
Catalina

Here and There (*Collection of Short Stories*)
Quartet (*Four Short Stories with Film Scripts*)
A Writer's Notebook
Trio (*Three Short Stories with Film Scripts*)
The Complete Short Stories (*3 Vols.*)
Encore (*Three Short Stories with Film Scripts*)
The Vagrant Mood
The Collected Plays (*3 Vols.*)
The Selected Novels (*3 Vols.*)
The Partial View
Ten Novels and Their Authors
The Travel Books

INTERMEDIATE LEVEL

Shane *by Jack Schaefer*
Old Mali and the Boy *by D. R. Sherman*
Bristol Murder *by Philip Prowse*
Tales of Goha *by Leslie Caplan*
The Smuggler *by Piers Plowright*
The Pearl *by John Steinbeck*
Things Fall Apart *by Chinua Achebe*
The Woman Who Disappeared *by Philip Prowse*
The Moon is Down *by John Steinbeck*
A Town Like Alice *by Nevil Shute*
The Queen of Death *by John Milne*
Walkabout *by James Vance Marshall*
Meet Me in Istanbul *by Richard Chisholm*
The Great Gatsby *by F. Scott Fitzgerald*
The Space Invaders *by Geoffrey Matthews*
My Cousin Rachel *by Daphne du Maurier*
I'm the King of the Castle *by Susan Hill*
Dracula *by Bram Stoker*
The Sign of Four *by Sir Arthur Conan Doyle*
The Speckled Band and Other Stories *by Sir Arthur Conan Doyle*
The Eye of the Tiger *by Wilbur Smith*
The Queen of Spades and Other Stories *by Aleksandr Pushkin*
The Diamond Hunters *by Wilbur Smith*
When Rain Clouds Gather *by Bessie Head*
Banker *by Dick Francis*
No Longer at Ease *by Chinua Achebe*
The Franchise Affair *by Josephine Tey*
The Case of the Lonely Lady *by John Milne*

For further information on the full selection of
Readers at all five levels in the series, please refer
to the Heinemann Guided Readers catalogue.

Heinemann International
A division of Heinemann Publishers (Oxford) Ltd
Halley Court, Jordan Hill, Oxford OX2 8EJ

OXFORD LONDON EDINBURGH
MADRID ATHENS BOLOGNA PARIS
MELBOURNE SYDNEY AUCKLAND SINGAPORE TOKYO
IBADAN NAIROBI HARARE GABORONE
PORTSMOUTH (NH)

ISBN 0 435 27221 7

Footprints in the Jungle was first published by William Heinemann Ltd in
1947, and *The Taipan* in 1921 and included in the *Complete Short Stories of
W. Somerset Maugham* (three volumes). *Giulia Lazzari* was first published by
William Heinemann Ltd in 1928 in a collection of stories entitled *Ashenden*.
These retold versions for Heinemann Guided Readers
© Rod Sinclair 1975, 1992
First published 1975
Reprinted eight times
This edition published 1992

Typography by Adrian Hodgkins
Cover by Janet Woolley and Threefold Design
Typeset in 11/12.5 pt Goudy
by Joshua Associates Ltd, Oxford
Printed and bound in Malta

92 93 94 95 96 97 10 9 8 7 6 5 4 3 2 1